GOOD NEWS

FOR

TODAY'S BUSINESS

I0391395

Nguzo C. Uche

ISBN-13: 978-1541104846
ISBN-10: 1541104846
Published by AMARHE Press
Printed by CreateSpace USA, An Amazon Company
eStore address: www.createspace.com/6793028

DEDICATION

This book is dedicated to those who quest for business success based on principles in the word of God. Also, to my entire family for their undeniable support. Finally, to all that have added value to my life, network group and beyond, I love you all.

.

CONTENTS

WHAT PEOPLE ARE SAYING ABOUT
Good News for Today's Business

Another great work from the author of the bestselling Title, "God's Legal Tender." This well-researched, well arranged and informative masterpiece is a must for every business manager, or entrepreneur, who wants to be successful.

------ Dr. Bennett Obi
Author and MD Rex Medical Center Lesotho

A new Composition has been born for prospective Business Partners, both old and new by this great author. The book is rich and anchors its strength in the word of God, the Holy Bible and this is good for all who actually want to succeed in business.

------ Dr. Louis Ngozi Ekezie
Alvan Ikoku Owerri, Nigeria

Good News for Today's Business underscores the importance of applying godly principles in business. Following the timeless and simple Biblical principles expounded in this book guarantees sustained success corporately and individually.

------ Pastor E.T Appiadu (CIMA, ADMA)
Facilitator University of Free State, South Africa.

VALUE OF BIBLE AND BUSINESS

The only business book that guarantees equity and integrity to business success is the Bible when properly applied. When you think of business, think about the word of God. As Strive Masiyiwa asserts "My favorite business book is the bible. If you study the bible with a view to extracting principles on how to set up, and manage a business effectively, you will be absolutely amazed; it has everything." Therefore, there is a surety in God's word if you know how to apply it.

BUSINESS

An organization or entity engaged in the provision of goods and services to customers/clients with the intent to making profit through service and value creation. Customers are the judge in the business value creation. An entrepreneur is the driver in business process and it flows from goal or objective definitions to its realization. "Price is what you pay. Value is what you get" says Warren Buffett. When business managers exceed the expectations of their customers through branding and rebranding of their service offering in a structured manner, value is created. What do your customers get, price or value?

INTRODUCTION

To work as an entrepreneur or employee in today's business environment saddled with challenges have become primary concern to global business success. Books represent a deep inner dialogue between the unseen (the author) and others privileged to get hold of it irrespective of the location and time lag.

Therefore, balancing business equation with the word of God is subtle in its totality. It is based on this that Good News for Today's Business was written in its simple terms to bridge the gap.

Business owners/managers and employees are business drivers with customers/clients as passengers and co-drivers with the same destination in mind. That is, value creation, delivery and judgment being the ultimate goal. Business ethics and integrity can only be achieved when sound biblical principles are applied. Every page in this book contains irrefutable Biblical principle developed in a structured manner to solve business and management problems. Customers' and employees' satisfaction count first .

DELIBERATING OVER PAST BUSINESS FAILURES

Isaiah 43:18-19

In business and life in general the number of times you fail is inconsequential. Deliberating over it adds no value because you are not working to get it right once. Never be ashamed by your business mistakes rather be a leaner and learn from the mistakes as learning is a continuous process.

NEVER SUBMIT TO PAST FAILURES

"Do not [earnestly] remember the former things; neither consider the things of old." Isaiah 43:18-19

Honesty is the watch word for every person to live by. At one time or the other we have all failed at different levels of our businesses. Only very few have learnt how to pick-up themselves and move on while many have not.

Interestingly, you and I have to learn from our failures or mistakes in business so that it does not repeat itself again. Don't be daunted in anyway because what failed is not you as a person but is the event, the action or business you undertook. Keep being focused and look ahead for better opportunities, it's brighter than imagined.

It is important to develop plans and priorities to overcome simple and common obstacles that hinder progress. Certainly, it costs much resources to pay for the same obnoxious business experience twice or more. Always follow plan with passion, navigate strategies and monitor momentum and progress for every step taken on the way.

Be confident today because you have learnt from your past; it will not repeat itself as long as you remain resolute. Today is full of business opportunities and possibilities to accomplish big things to him that believes. Every morning say goodbye to yesterday's mistakes and failures and welcome the new day with good morning and big cheers.

Businesses make mistakes and fail. How often have you as a business owner or management picked-up yourself and forgot the past? There must always be a time of business crisis, the way you handle it determines your survival and success. Proverb 24:16 says "For a righteous man falls seven times and rises again." Remarkably, falling is not the issue but the ability to rise is the primary concern.

The good news is "a righteous man" definitely must rise again if he wills. Are you a righteous man? If you are, there is hope for you and your business to bounce back, shake off the past. Colonel Sanders says "One has to remember that every failure can be a stepping-stone to something better." Now, do you still consider past failures?

UNDERSTANDING BUSINESS PHILOSOPHY

Joshua 1:10-11

When right people are engaged in the right place with right business collaboration, business competence, productivity and growth emerge. Dynamic debate unveils business philosophy.

TEAM BUSINESS STRATEGIES AND PLANNING

"Then Joshua commanded the officers of the people, saying, pass through the camp and command the people, Prepare your provisions, for within three days you shall pass over this Jordan to go in to take possession of the land which the Lord your God is giving you to possess." Joshua 1:10-11

Joshua is one of the strategic leaders that had ever lived in his time. Examine his discourse, at the right season and apt time to possess the land promised by God. His strategic options were concise and clear on how his team should organize for action. The what, how, when, where and tactics were spelt out to the informed and collaborative team.

Therefore, in your business or organization no matter the position you may occupy, try and apply Joshua's strategic approach with your team if you have any. At the right and set time for business opportunity brainstorm with the team, state the objective, define what they should do as team not individually and time-box the delivery of the stated business objective. Also, let the action commence as unanimously agreed without interruption.

Remember, the moment project objective is clear and the team is self-organized and collaborative, it takes little or nothing to follow-up. The ultimate thing is, you watch the team deliver key project deliverables in short time. Proverb 8:6 says "Hear, for I will speak excellent {and} princely things; and the opening of my lips shall be for right things." Therefore, when excellent and right preparations are made, the team produces right results.

Progressive and effective leaders do not micro-manage a team. Command, control and allocation of duties are not effective in a self-organized or self-managed team for business value to be delivered. Does your team/employee understand your business philosophy? Therefore, if they don't, this is the time for you to reorganize for better business deals.

SOLVING CUSTOMERS' CONCERNS

1 Samuel 8:19

Customers are the judge in every business value delivered and solving their problems promptly guarantee their commitment and loyalty.

LISTEN TO CUSTOMERS CONCERNS

"So listen now to their voice; only solemnly warn them and show them the ways of the king who shall reign over them." 1 Samuel 8:19

The dividends of live are tied to a process of time. Everything that had ever happened in our office, organization, church and business took a long time and not accidental. It is only we failed to listen and recognize it at first.

Business customers/clients do not precipitously disappear or change loyalty without reasons; they do have one or more. In our quest for profit maximization we unknowingly ignore the signal/s of dissatisfactions of our customers, employees and even the church congregation where applicable before they sort alternative elsewhere. Phil Libin says, "Feedback is great for telling you what you did wrong. It's terrible at telling you what you should do next."

To pay sincere attention to complaints and concerns of customers is the starting point of keeping or retaining their loyalty and patronage. Whatever feedback that comes from internal (employees) or external customers/clients should be given much attention irrespective of how undesirable it sounds to us. As a leader or manager be committed to addressing the problem/s wholeheartedly. Even when the customers are irrational, express outright regret of their actions and ask how you might help resolve their concerns.

Take charge in resolving customers' issues, follow them up through any means to reassure confidence in them and maintain their ultimate satisfaction and loyalty at large. Proverb 12:8 says "A man shall be commended according to his Wisdom [godly Wisdom, which is comprehensive insight into the ways and purposes of God], but he who is of a perverse heart shall be despised." Thriving of any business requires wisdom and understanding of the business language in context.

Therefore, is pertinent to purposefully attend to complaints and bitterness when they are small than to allow them to magnify. It pays to do so than losing your customers. Prompt response to complaints should be the business value for customers, employees and others around the business to be happy in order to enjoy their support. Happiness is relative; seek for what makes your customers happy. Do you solve your customers'/employees' problems? Whichever side your answer falls better revisit your business before it goes down.

VALUE OF BUSINESS COMPETITION

Luke 14:28, 31

Business innovation/re-engineering is the product of industry competition for effective and efficient service delivery.

DISCERN YOUR COMPETITORS

"For which of you, wishing to build a farm building, does not first sit down and calculate the cost [to see] whether he has sufficient means to finish it? Or what king, going out to engage in conflict with another king, will not first sit down and consider {and} take counsel whether he is able with ten thousand [men] to meet him who comes against him with twenty thousand?" Luke 14:28, 31

The Bible has been a good management book beyond its intended use. It stated above "calculate the cost," then it is necessary to consider and reconsider business competitors through feasibility study when starting a business or increasing business portfolio. As important as that may be, calculating the cost of business allows the opportunity to appraise the competitive nature of the business environment in order to be strategically positioned.

The cost of business starts from having a good business plan and feasibility study. The business plan avails the golden opportunity to know the initial business capital and cash flow needed to sustain the business, the necessary resources, like manpower, equipment and possibly the market share envisaged.

Note, no matter how big or small your business or outfit may be, always count the cost, analyze your personal strength and weakness to sustain the business with your competitors. The Scripture says, "For by wise counsel you can wage your war, and in an abundance of counselors there is victory {and} safety," Proverb 24:6. It takes wise counsel to win war; wise counsel, and good preparation to compete and win in any business environment.

Remember, every little mistake has a cost attached to it and it might be very outrageous and unbearable to contend. Stephen Covey says, "When you pick one end of a stick the other end is picked too." In other words, every decision has a corresponding consequence attached to it. Therefore, it is unfair for a man to build a house without knowing what it will take. Always consider your big or small competitors and anticipated business entrants when venturing into anything that requires financial commitment. Do you consider competitors when opening a business? Even though they may seem irrelevant to your business they can put you out of business. Reconsider their strengths and weaknesses in a professional manner.

EFFECTS OF FUND IN BUSINESS

Habakkuk 2:7

The pathetic thing that destroys business is lack of cash and its mismanagement. Money is the pivot and oil that lubricate business if managed well.

LENDERS AND BUSINESS INFLUENCE

"Won't your creditors revolt unexpectedly? Won't those who make you tremble wake up? As a result, you'll become their prey," Habakkuk 2:7 ISV.

Many businesses started with loan from one source or the other. The Scripture says, won't your creditors revolt unexpectedly and you will become their prey. As interesting as it may sound, there is no boundary to where loan could be obtained to run a business rather there is inherent implication of unexpected revolt of creditors in the near future.

Expanding business, making capital or current expenditures with loan is not bad; make sure someone pays for it. Every businessman should be wise and proactive. Before making any financial commitment for loan, understand the terms and conditions inserted in the agreement. Where possible solicit for professional advice. Also, consider if your business would be able to payback in a short possible time when needed. Honesty and sincerity should guide you when borrowing.

Every loan from any source has a due date and truthfully if your return on investment (ROI) is negative the loan is needless to avoid embarrassment. One thing is paramount, lenders can ask for their money when things seem rough and unpredictable. They have the ability and all resources to confiscate your assets in a minute before your eyes when terms and conditions are breached. Someone describes them as "people that offer umbrella when the sun is up and quickly collect it as soon as the rain comes." "The rich rule over the poor, and the borrower is servant to the lender," Proverb 22:7. As a debtor the level of control you have over your business is small because of your limited capital investment. When you borrow, definitely you are a servant to the lender. Be a wise debtor. What percentage of control do you have over your business? If your control is small then reassess the terms and conditions of your loan.

TEAM COMMUNICATION

Nehemiah 2:17

In non-team work environment where confidential communication is discouraged, workers sabotage their leaders when problems show forth if they have 'them vs. us' mindset.

COLLABORATE WITH YOUR WORKERS

"Then I said to them, you see the bad situation we are in--how Jerusalem lies in ruins, and its gates are burned with fire. Come, let us build up the wall of Jerusalem, that we may no longer be a disgrace."
Nehemiah 2:17

No business or organization has ever being without one crisis or the other. Leadership is about communication. When time of trouble and hard time show up in your organization how do you interconnect with your workers? Openness and honesty are paramount when dealing with workers/staff. There is a great need to explain to them the circumstance and issues on the table and together you can find solution that will make them to take ownership; that is team work.

When you cannot pay salaries or keep to the promises made to staff, let them know the why. Anytime the company is in difficulty the management, staff and other business stakeholders are experiencing its negative effects together.

As a leader or manager effectively communicate to everyone and allow them proffer solution to the problem. The moment there is clarification and the workers feel valued they tend to work as self-organized and self-motivated team to resolve issues even in your absence.

Workers sabotage their leaders when problems show forth if they have the sense of 'them vs. us' mentality. The Bible says, "A friend loves at all times and a brother is always there to help at the bad times" Proverb 17:17 EasyEnglish. Customers and suppliers may go but your staff may have something to offer when effectively communicated. Always bridge the gap and be on the same page with them. Are you on the same page with your workers? It pays to collaborate with staff.

HASTY BUSINESS SUCCESS

Deuteronomy 7:22

Business breakthrough is assured when diligence and skillfulness are coordinated for a definite outcome. Customers' relationship and referrals are the key factors.

HASTY FOR OVERNIGHT BREAKTHROUGH

"And the Lord your God will clear out those nations before you, little by little; you may not consume them quickly," Deuteronomy 7:22

Our God is an awesome God; He believes in process, incremental and progress over time. Every business that has survived and got breakthrough came only when effort, time and comprehensive work package have been packaged and delivered in a more professional manner. "God will clear out those nations before you, little by little." In other words, success trickles in little by little not overnight.

It is only once in a long while one might get a chance of overnight breakthrough happening in business and life in general. Relationship is the major key factor in business success. How often do you reply emails, return voicemails, missed phone calls from customers/associates? What about your business promises, do you keep them? Do you honor warranty and guarantee given to customers? What about customers/employees complain, do you attend to them promptly? All count for business success.

Remember, "Little drops of water make mighty river." When you do little things right and at the right time the business will grow and breakthrough will spring forth. Proverb 22:29 says, "Do you see a man diligent {and} skillful in his business? He will stand before kings; he will not stand before obscure men." Business breakthrough is assured when diligence and skillfulness are coordinated for a definite outcome. Being anxious to see swift business success leads to misconduct and failure. Business breakthrough is a process and it takes time. Are you hasty for business breakthrough? Remember, successful businesses around the world like Microsoft, Apple Computer, Amazon, Dangote, and others took years to build their business breakthrough. "Wealth, like happiness, is never attained when sought after directly. It comes as a by-product of providing a useful service," says Colonel Sanders.

BUSINESS TOOLS AND TECHNIQUES

Ecclesiastes 10:10

Every business dies when it stops innovating, if you want to grow, determine a new path of growth curve outside the accepted business average. As technology changes, companies, organizations and businesses need to update in order to remain relevant in the industry. When you stop thinking, you stop innovating.

USE OF OLD TECHNOLOGY

"If the ax is dull and the man does not whet the edge, he must put forth more strength; but wisdom helps him to succeed." Ecclesiastes 10:10

Many that may have used dull ax to cut wood will testify that more energy, time and strength are needed to accomplish the task. World over, the moment business tools, techniques and skills are non-operational and obsolete, productivity suffers and general satisfaction declines.

Wisdom is the principal thing; and it gives business success if properly applied. As technology changes, companies, organizations and businesses need to update in order to remain relevant in the industry. Make a comprehensive inventory of your business resources even the staff to see if they are relevant for the job or not. Continuous improvement and evaluation of all business resources will help business to remain competitive.

No person will like to work with dull ax or tool; staff

morale and business profitability are tied to sharpened and working tools. The Bible explicitly says, "Be diligent to know the state of your flocks, and look well to your herds;" Proverb 27:23. If the condition/s of the flocks is unknown they might die unexpectedly. Therefore, pay close attention, some of your staff may no longer be relevant to your business, train them where necessary, if not get rid of them. Do you still work with obsolete technology and techniques? Dave Lazor says, "Sometimes, a new technological investment is just what you need for future business success. A Microsoft study concluded that more than 90% of consumers would consider taking their business elsewhere rather than work with a company that used outdated technology-dial-up internet, Windows 98, etc." Sharpen your dull ax, upgrade to new business friendly technology.

NON-PRODUCING BUSINESS

Luke 13:7

When you keep worthless resources hanging on, it signifies lack of business competence and understanding.

NON-PRODUCING BUSINESS/DEPARTMENT

"So he said to the vinedresser, See here! For these three years I have come looking for fruit on this fig tree and I find none. Cut it down! Why should it continue also to use up the ground [to deplete the soil, intercept the sun, and take up room]?" Luke 13:7

"Cut it down!" or downsize is a very difficult decision to make in business by many if not all. The Fig tree's performance is contrary to the expectation of the owner. Therefore, critical decision and a very hard one is needed to bring it down.

Every critical business investment requires critical and expensive decision about cutting down the resources and the losses going down the drain over years. It is interesting to know that most business plans are well put together by experts, implemented by professionals and financed by the best financial institutions in the state; often times they fail or fall below the predetermined objectives and expectations of the business sponsors.

The hard nut to crack is when to say it is over, let's cut it down. Most departments in the public sector and government projects are no longer productive, time and money are being wasted to keep them running. Also, in our private businesses we borrow money to keep business that has negative return on investment. Cut it down my dear, why must it use up the space?

Every well thought out business has a payback period. Business objective must be clear and precise; if it cannot yield its objective over a period take a decision to cut it down. The Scripture asserts, "He who tills his land shall be satisfied with bread, but he who follows worthless pursuits is lacking in sense {and} is without understanding" Proverb 12:11. When you keep worthless resources hanging on, it signifies lack of business competence and understanding. Non-producing business/department or resources is like pouring water in a bottomless tank/pit and expect it to get full. Are you hanging on with non-producing business?

ALL KNOWING MANAGER

Ecclesiastes 4:13

Don't impose your predetermined ideas on people that will make them intimidated and inferior. Ego destroys business leader.

THE KNOW ALL BUSINESS BOSS

"Better is a poor and wise youth than an old and foolish king who no longer knows how to receive counsel (friendly reproof and warning)"
Ecclesiastes 4:13

Business management is a synergy of collaboration of efforts and resources. There are individual areas of dominance and specialization. Position does not equal universal experience and wisdom. Subordinates and colleagues have roles to play in the business management. Their inputs count a lot if you still need to be effective.

Most businesses have come and gone before the eyes of their owners/leaders. They sometimes or most of the time assume they have solution to every problem. Good managers leverage on the strength of others working with them. The rank and file may have the right answers when consulted. Never ignore people just because you lead them. John C. Maxwell said, "In my organization I don't have employees; I have teammates. Yes, I do pay people and offer them benefits. But people don't work for me. They work with me. We are working together to fulfill the vision. Without them, I cannot succeed." 'He that is very close to the mouth says exactly how it smells.' Workers in the field have better knowledge, understanding and picture of the situation.

No suggestion should be thrown away rather appreciate it; evaluate its relevance in the subject matter and reward the individual or group of individuals for the effort. This makes people feel valued in the workplace. Don't impose your predetermined ideas on people that will make them intimidated and inferior. The idea of knowing more than others which Geoff Marlow asserts "It leads to a vicious circle where influential people inadvertently create conditions that block the ability in others to cooperate and collaborate to co-create a better future." "By pride {and} insolence comes only contention, but with the well-advised is skillful {and} godly Wisdom" Proverb 13:10. The Lord elbows the pride and contention will always exist if you   are a proud leader/manager.

Inspire them, I mean your subordinates, colleagues and others to work with you as a team. No idea is a waste until proven not feasible. When you do all, you invite stress and burnout into your life. Are you boss know all? Then if you are, sit back and evaluate what it has caused you and the business. People always refrain working with an egocentric leader. Examine yourself and get along.

WORKPLACE GENDER BIAS

Proverb 2:9

Women play vital role in the workplace and they should be hired so long as they are qualified for the position. They do not belong to our assumptions.

OFFICE GENDER EQUALITY

"Then you will understand righteousness, justice, and fair dealing [in every area and relation]; yes, you will understand every good path." Proverb 2:9

Over the years, United Nation, Human Right groups and other Activist groups globally are agitating for gender equality in all sphere of life. As a business owner or manager the bible says, understand righteousness, justice and equity in whatever you do. Notwithstanding our standpoint on gender in the workplace and women to be precise; justice and equality should be the overriding factors. Balancing recruitment and promotion equation support business growth and success.

Women play vital role in the workplace and they should be hired so long as they are qualified for the position. The idea of exclusive job position/s for men in the office should not exist if you want to grow as God wants you. Many women across the entire continents of the world have proved themselves competent in many areas in their respective industries. Undoubtedly, the marginalization continues to evolve in the minds of many business owners and managers.

The Bible puts it this way, "to show partiality is not good." Therefore, to avoid being partial in the recruitment process, the picture of work description, qualification, merit for promotion, rewards, punishment and dismissal etc. should be spelt out from the onset. In hiring let the best candidate be employed irrespective of ones gender inclination.

The moment equity, justice and righteousness become our watch word while hiring and promoting employees we'll hit the road to growth and success. Are you gender biased? Relatively if you are, there is great need to retrace for you have failed the law of righteousness, justice, and fair dealing in every area and relation in business. For in God's law, if one is failed you have failed all.

INVESTMENT IN WORKERS

2 Corinthians 9:6

The most valuable economic development an organization can implement is investment in workers. They are the first key to the business growth than the tools, resources and other factors of production money is being spent on daily basis.

THE MOST VALUABLE BUSINESS ASSET

"[Remember] this: he who sows sparingly {and} grudgingly will also reap sparingly {and} grudgingly, and he who sows generously [that blessings may come to someone] will also reap generously {and} with blessings." 2 Corinthians 9:6

The most valuable asset in business and organization is the people (staff) that do the work. They are the first key to the business growth than the tools, resources and other factors of production money is being spent on daily basis. Some business owners/managers have ignored human capital development so much so the organization suffers.

In business, no matter how small it may be, train the staff. How often have you trained the new employees? More often than not there is no provision to take them through orientation in the workplace. The business mission, vision, objectives, tactics and values are not communicated. Out there you hear employers say 'come and start work the next day,' sometimes on phone that's all. No customer relationship management training. Some businesses exhibit animals from the zoo as staff. Above all, much is expected of them.

No one performs effectively where there is no adequate training. Let your staff understand your business philosophy, interaction with customers, suppliers and the community where you operate. It adds to production and decision efficiency. More importantly, let there be a forum or safe atmosphere to ask question/s when in doubt. If you want your business to be more productive and effective, develop your workers. According to John C. Maxwell, "The bottom line in leadership isn't how far we advance ourselves but how far we advance others." On that note, investing in human capital takes a process, money and energy to come by. But if you sow sparingly {and} grudgingly in your workers capacity building; you will also reap sparingly {and} grudgingly from their contribution and output.

The moment employees are properly trained for the job; productivity and growth will show forth in the organization.

Do you disinvest in your workers? There are always business consequences to lack of capacity building. Redirect your investment today.

CONSEQUENCE OF COMFORT ZONE

Deuteronomy 2:2-3

Anyone that enjoys comfort zone will not make progress and there will be no innovation and competitiveness in the business. There is no single road to arrive to a business destination.

BUSINESS COMFORT ZONE

Then the Lord said to me (Moses), "You have walked round this hill for a long time. Now turn to the north" Deuteronomy 2:2-3 EasyEnglish.

Frankly, repeating one business concept over many years with great expectation of a different business outcome is unacceptable. Business comfort zone is the most dangerous place to hide when progress is not made. Anytime much investment has been given to an idea, thought and business plan and no result, find an alternative. Most often our established practices may have been overtaken by innovations and technologies. Many of us still operate with the concept 'as it was in the past so shall it be now and forever.' Only God will be until the end of time.

Gold and diamond are never found on surface but you need to dig deeper with changes in technology. There is no single road to arrive to a business destination. If business location/premises is not favorable change the place. Don't use the low rent you pay to kill the business. Never allow fear of failure and perfectionism to deter you.

The only thing that is constant is change. If you are not attuned to change and catch up with the trend your business will go down. Moses and his people walked around the hill for so long waiting for a miracle or breakthrough, but the Lord cautioned him to break status quo and change direction. Many business owners and managers have circled around one business idea for a long time without results or anything to show forth. It is time for you to rethink, change your methodology, and develop big business ideas in context for you to rule your world. Determine your north today and turn toward it for business success. Anyone that enjoys comfort zone will not make progress and there will be no innovation and competitiveness in the business.

The Scripture says, "When you walk, your steps shall not be hampered [your path will be clear and open]; and when you run, you shall not stumble" Proverb 4:12. As you step out of the business/life comfort zone with faith; the Lord has assured your steps will not be hampered nor stumbled but every decision/s will be open and clear for good results. Do you enjoy your comfort zone? Your answer is better than my imagination. If you are, better navigate to your north today for business success.

ACTIVE BUSINESS LISTENER

James 1:19

Listening is the key in business meetings and other conversations, when ignored leadership is destined to fail.

THE NEED TO LISTEN WELL

"Understand [this], my beloved brethren. Let every man be quick to hear [a ready listener], slow to speak, slow to take offense {and} to get angry."
James 1:19

All business engagements revolve around communication. Organizations and businesses spend about 90% of their time communicating. However, any communication without a clear purpose is simply an interaction.

Listening is the key in business meetings and other interactions. The Bible says, don't be quick to speak or talk but be quick to hear (listen). Good listeners make great impact in the organization. Allow people to air their views from their own standpoint in meetings and other communications. Take time to listen.

In every business meeting and communication with customers, suppliers, and other stakeholders always listen and then present logical and constructive points relevant to the subject. Make presentations with facts, figures, illustrations and references. Listen with the intent to understand every aspect of the conversation before you contribute.

Listen! for I will speak noble things says the Lord. Therefore, if you don't listen to understand you will miss the noble things. Effective listening is a vital factor in business. As business owners/managers, listen to your staff than shouting them down. When you do so, unspoken words could be figured out. Are you a good listener? As a staff listen to your boss and customers before you act or respond. Don't jump into conclusion when issues are being reported. Be a good listener.

BORING BUSINESS MEETING

1 Corinthians 9:26

Most office meetings are routine and tradition with no clear objective to achieve business goal.

CONDUCTING AN EFFECTIVE MEETING

"That is the way I run, with a clear goal in mind. That is the way I fight, not like someone shadow boxing" 1 Corinthians 9:26 ISV.

Too many meetings conducted in the office or for business purposes fail to achieve their aims. In planning meetings, attendees move from one point to the other without achieving any tangible thing at the end. Most of these meetings are office routine or ritual meetings without any goal. That is, 'today being Monday our meeting is from 8am to 9am.' This is office tradition with no urgent goal.

Every scheduled business or administrative meeting must be important and urgent with clear cut agenda. Some people attend meetings making constructive and intelligent suggestions and decisions to resolve organizational problems. Others go with selfish aim in mind like playing office or departmental politics, to take tea or lunch and to make their voices heard etc.

Beforehand determine the meeting agenda, objective/s, time, location and the relevant participants. Where possible provide everyone with a written agenda. Every meeting should be brief; stand-up meeting is very effective.

In other to save time when attending meetings, participants should be prompt, prepared, involved, attentive, relevant, and brief with their contribution. They should be courteous and focus on issues not individuals. Meetings should not stretch more than necessary; let it be time-boxed to avoid non related points overshadowing the purpose.

Effective meeting produces efficiency and productivity in an organization. Have you been in a boring meeting? Think for a better solution to reorganize your business or organization to be effective in every business meeting.

WISHING FOR BUSINESS OPPORTUNITY

Amos 3:5

Business success trickles in after some measurable efforts must have gone in. Customers refer friends and associates to the business after they may have established confidence based on their past experiences.

SOURCE FOR BUSINESS BEYOND

"Can a bird fall in a snare upon the earth where there is no trap for him? Does a trap spring up from the ground when nothing at all has sprung it?"
Amos 3:5

No! That does not happen; there must be a cause for every action. Business opportunities are not wished in to the office.

Business success trickles in after some measurable efforts must have gone in. No business opportunity has ever flown in to the office without some deliberate and calculated effort by the operator/s. Customer relationship management, advertisement and business sourcing count a lot for potential opportunities to stroll in to the office.

Customers refer friends and associates to the business after they may have established confidence based on their past experiences. In the age we live today, reaching out to customers and the potential ones are easier due to technology. The birth of internet and the social media platforms have helped in business traffic. The use of Facebook, Twitter, Whatsapp, Goggle, LinkedIn and many others are welcome development in the business world. Business operators need to be in front of their customers always to keep them in their business corridor. Online marketing platforms are vital to bring in business opportunities. Owners and managers of business should embrace the use of ebay.com, amazon.com, alibaba.com, Jumia.com etc. notwithstanding the size of business.

Importantly, some business strategies may have gone obsolete and need to be reevaluated. Every business time and money should be channeled to current methodologies to attract customers and good businesses. Wining new businesses and customers take some resources and intensive advertisement to achieve. Therefore, for any business barn to be filled with plenty opportunities, customers and businesses should be systematically and intentionally looked for and retained. Never wait for customers and businesses to come looking for you; they will not because there are many that had gone out for them. Do you sit and pray for business to come? If yes, stand up, shake off the cold and go out and negotiate for good business deals with potential customers out there.

BUSINESS SUCCESSION

1 Chronicles 23:1

Business legacy strictly depends on well trained successor who will flag the business at the departure of the owner.

BUILD A BUSINESS SUCCESSOR

"WHEN DAVID was old and full of days, he made Solomon his son king over Israel." 1 Chronicles 23:1

The continuity of business from one leadership or generation to another should be one of the prime factors to be considered from inception. No single individual is immortal and indispensible. Some business leaders, managers and all of us to a large extent act as if they will not get old and eventually give up to ghost one day. Many wonderful businesses have come and gone as their owners depart the earth because there was no formal succession blueprint or "pass it on" program.

Remember when David was about to die he trained and made Solomon the King over Israel. Also, Elijah trained Elisha as a successor. This is a succession strategy. When a business owner trains a competent successor he indirectly averts the in-house fighting and destruction of the business. Confusion always show forth when we finally drop dead which is inevitable.

Let's face the truth, no one lives forever but with wisdom and knowledge one can plan for the future. King Hezekiah was asked to set his house in order for he shall not live. Therefore, set your business in order for you may not know tomorrow. Make the right plan because your business legacy strictly depends on your well trained and competent successor who will flag the business at your departure when it pleases your creator.

Ultimately, the Bible says, the naïve acquire folly, but the prudent are crowned with knowledge. Have you any plan for your successor? Where there is one, this is the time to roll it out. Start the training process and don't wait till the last day. The only way to know that you ever owned or managed a business is it's continuity after you must have gone. "A leader's lasting value is measured by succession."

STOCK MANAGEMENT

Ezra 8:34

Prudent managers take careful inventory of their business stock and keep accurate records in every business transaction to uphold stakeholders' trust.

KEEP BUSINESS INVENTORY

"Every piece was counted and weighed, and all the weight was recorded at once." Ezra 8:34

One of the driving forces for every business is to maximize profit. This could only be achieved when prudent accounting process or system is in place. The scripture above says, everything was numbered and weighted. In others words, business should keep in and out inventory of stock.

Good inventory management system enhances business profitability. At the beginning and end of every business day proper balancing of stock should be conducted. Shortages in stock should be resolved in order to know what happened and to avoid its recurrences. Never overlook little stock shortages as they are part of the overall business investments. All little losses magnify into big amount that would have been the business profit.

There are too many inventory management software like InFlow, Fishbowl, Inventory Tracker Plus,

Contalog etc. available in the shops to help track goods in and out. Inventory management must be a collaborative effort of the staff. Cameras should be installed in and around the business premises to monitor the activities of people. Also, as a manager never take any item out of your shop without keeping a record or paying for it. This attitude may cause your staff to do the same and the business to lose profit.

Therefore, if proper inventory management and tracking system are in control, the business will reduce losses and build profit. How often do you take stock inventory? Business profits are wrapped around the stock. Any stock that got lost and not traced steps the business an inch backward. Retrain yourself and staff on inventory management.

PROMPT RESPONSE IN BUSINESS

Ezekiel 33:6

Dynamic organizations create an environment where people genuinely speak up about an issue that might affect their work section or department on time without being victimized.

PROMPT REPORTING OF PROBLEMS

"But if the watchman sees the sword coming and does not blow the trumpet and the people are not warned, and the sword comes and takes any one of them, he is taken away in {and} for his perversity {and} iniquity, but his blood will I require at the watchman's hand." Ezekiel 33:6

The success of every business is a collective responsibility of all. The management has the duty to raise alarm when there is a problem and likewise the rank and file.

As a staff, it is good for you to inform the authority about the problem in your line of duty or department before it escalates. The supervisor, manager, or team leader needs to be notified. Always be courageous and strong to tell the truth before your supervisor about an issue in the office even when the platform weren't created by the management.

The scripture says if the watchman sees sword coming and fails to notify the people their blood will be required of him. Therefore, as a worker no matter your position when you fail to inform the management about the problem you envisaged; you will be held responsible for its consequences. Have you ever been punished for not reporting problems in your section which ought to have been rectified before they got out of hand? If yes, change your approach and be committed.

On the other hand, management should create an enabling ground for workers to speak up. In some organizations when people genuinely speak up about an issue that might affect their work section or department, they are victimized. This kind of attitude jeopardizes the organizational or business growth.

Business owners should be open and sincere to their workers for them to point out problems as early as possible. Staff willingness and boldness to do so increase the overall performance of the company. Do you see things and allow it to degenerate?

CONSEQUENCES OF ARROGANCE

Deuteronomy 8:18

Our initial disposition in any communication determines the response we receive; therefore respect people's views and opinions even when they fall short of your expectation.

DON'T BE ARROGANT IN BUSINESS

"But you shall [earnestly] remember the Lord your God, for it is He Who gives you power to get wealth that He may establish His covenant which He swore to your fathers, as it is this day." Deuteronomy 8:18

Human beings inadvertently become arrogant when they see changes in their social and economic status. Someone once said "arrogance equals ego plus ignorance and little money." Some business owners and entrepreneurs display signs of arrogance in the manner and ways they relate with staff, customers and suppliers at large. It takes confidence and determination to be successful in business. Always remember that the ability and the flow of wealth come from above. The wealth and success in business are not by personal efforts rather is a confirmation of God's covenant.

The Bible acknowledged that God hates the proud. Remember that the wealthy man in the Bible that was arrogant with the success of his business and what he has done by his own strength; that night his life was taken from him. Arrogance can't take you far and it destroys business efforts. Are you arrogant in your business? Have you ever asked your staff or friends if they know how you made it? You made it is not by your power rather is God that gave you power to get wealth that He may establish His covenant.

BUSINESS IS A SERVICE

1 Peter 4:10

To make our customers happy we need to improve collaboration through feedback cycles, iterative and incremental delivery of products. Business is a service not only a profit maximization venture at the expense of the people.

EVERY BUSINESS IS A SERVICE

"Each of you should use whatever gift you have received to serve others, as faithful stewards of God's grace in its various forms" 1 Peter 4:10 NIV.

The first point of call or consideration when opening a business is to see it as service to others. Customers and clients pay for service you have rendered. The scripture says, you should use whatever gift you have received to serve others. In order words, use your training, skill and profession to serve others.

As a business owner, are your staff trained to render honest service to customers? Is your interest only to get money off their wallets? In the retail shop business, responses to customers complain and enquiries count a lot. Do you force people to pay for service/s you never provided? Many countries in Africa, customers are forced to pay for electricity bills they never used. Remember your business should serve others as faithful steward of God.

Business is about giving to get, investing to receive.

The Bible says, give it shall be given to you, good measure, press down, shaken together and running over. Always create good opportunity to give your best to customers first and they will sound the business trumpet for you. Treat your customers well. Take them as your extended family members because they are members of the business family. Business is a service not only a profit maximization venture at the expense of the people. Win-win strategy pays when you render service to customers. Do you see your business as service to others?

DISMAYED WITH BUSINESS IDEAS

Joshua 1:9

Business goals are achieved through persistent effort and willful confidence that you can achieve what you intended. Remain resolute for you are some meters away from the finish line.

SECRET OF AN ENTREPRENEUR

"Have not I commanded you? Be strong, vigorous, and very courageous. Be not afraid, neither be dismayed, for the Lord your God is with you wherever you go." Joshua 1:9

Being an entrepreneur is the dream of many individuals in the society. Entrepreneurs are the drivers of any economy and the most business risk takers. They are confident driven entities. This single factor holds many from starting a business and sustaining it.

The Lord said, be strong and courageous, do not be afraid and never be discouraged for He is with you. Therefore, be strong and courageous about your business, company and organization ideas as an entrepreneur. Every entrepreneur is not only selling his goods and services but himself. They believe in themselves to have all it takes to bring change/s. However, if one does not believe in himself, no one will believe in his products and services.

Jesus told them, "Don't be afraid; just believe" Mark 5:36. As a business owner there will be times when you will be the only person that believes in your business vision and plan. Don't be afraid; just believe. Be confident and push on your business idea.

Most successful entrepreneurs are confident, strong, courageous and vigorous in pushing their business ideas above and beyond the boundaries for they know that the LORD their God will be with them wherever they go. Be resolute and keep on pushing. Are you dismayed with your business ideas? If you are, you worth not to be an entrepreneur.

BUSINESS ACCOUNTABILITY

Luke 12:36

The abuse of office is a premeditated subversion of accountability. The only thing that makes Organizations to deliver on their promises is reputation.

BE PREPARED FOR ACCOUNTABILITY

"And be like men who are waiting for their master to return home from the marriage feast, so that when he returns from the wedding and comes and knocks, they may open to him immediately." Luke 12:36

We are informed that the Lord will come very soon and the time unknown to anyone. Therefore, there is urgent need to be prepared and wait. The scripture says, be like men who are waiting for their master to return and they may open the door for him. Be ready at all time.

Every business is subject to accountability. Internal and external audit should be randomly conducted. As a business operator or manager are you ready and willing to render account to the management when asked? The very moment you assume any responsibility in the office either private or public you are accountable to someone. The abuse of office is a premeditated subversion of accountability.

The primary function of staff is to be fully ready to

account for everything committed into their hands. Proper accountability makes one an efficient and effective worker to the employer. It is disheartening to see that many public office holders sabotage audit or deliberately refuse to give account of their stewardship.

Note that your immediate senior may call you to render account unannounced. Are you ready to do so? Would you give excuses because of your misconducts and inappropriate deals? Always be in control to respond to any call or demand for stewardship. Businesses prosper when someone in charge gives account and allows himself to be audited at any time. Be prepared to show yourself approved in the office. Are you willing to give account unannounced? If your response is no why must you take up responsibility you intend not to account for.

SUBSTANDARD PRODUCT DELIVERY

Proverbs 20:10

Excellent organizational plan or design does not guarantee excellent product and service delivery. Let your business value circles around quality product delivery.

Nguzo C. Uche

PRODUCT QUALITY ASSURANCE (PQA)

"Diverse weights [one for buying and another for selling] and diverse measures--both of them are exceedingly offensive {and} abhorrent to the Lord."
Proverbs 20:10

All growing businesses and companies maintain standards and quality. Quality assurance is their watch word. Every effort to keep to the demand of our customers should not undermine product quality.

The Scripture warns that differing weights and measures are abominable to the Lord. As serious as the warning may sound, differing weights is a breach of trust customers have on you and that of the business. The economic crunch in today's business may lead into cutting corners and substandard in products and services delivered to customers.

Anytime products are delivered to customers that did not meet defined quality standard you have failed. Maintain one standard for all customers and nations. Never produce certain product quality for developed

80

nations and substandard for the developing or poor nations.

Pride your business with quality. All the time conduct quality test on products you produce for customers. Any business that fails to keep standards and good scale will not prosper. Businesses grow when they build good reputation of quality standard over the years.

When you quote for a job, do you deliver exactly what you bided for? Do you deliver quality education as you promised the parents? "Can I justify wicked scales and a bag of deceptive weights" when dealing with customers. There is no justification for deceptive weights even when cost of production is high. Let your business value circles around quality product delivery. Do you deliver substandard products to customers?

WITHHOLDING VENDORS' PAYMENTS

Proverbs 3:27-28

The thin line between the buyer and the vendor is signature, as one determines the other person's joy and happiness when goods and services are delivered.

BE HONEST TO VENDORS/CONTRACTORS

"Withhold not good from those to whom it is due [its rightful owners], when it is in the power of your hand to do it. Do not say to your neighbor, Go, and come again; and tomorrow I will give it--when you have it with you." Proverbs 3:27-28

Business is a flow of interaction in a value stream. No single person can complete the business chain or circle in other to make profit. The interaction between the producers, wholesalers, retailers and final consumers are vital if kept active.

As a business owner, your management style and approach in paying your vendors and contractors should be of importance to you. Do you withhold payments due to your suppliers and contractors? The Scripture emphasized that withholding good from those to whom it is due is not good. The moment you enter into contract or agreement with contractors or suppliers try and keep to your own part. Never dig out reason/s why you will not pay after supply and contract have been accomplished. The suppliers are vital entities of your business chain. Asking vendors to come today or tomorrow when you have what is due to them is not acceptable in the presence of God and man. The moment bills are paid at the right time you prove yourself to be trustworthy for business.

Every businessman should understand this, "those who give freely gain even more; others hold back what they owe becoming even poorer" Proverbs 11:24 ISV. On that note, when you intentionally withhold the money or refuse to sign suppliers invoices your business will become poor. Desist from telling stories to your suppliers after they have done their part of the deal

For your business to grow, always fulfill your own part by paying as at when due. Do you withhold vendors' payments? If you don't, what about your workers' salaries? Investing workers' salaries in other things to make profit for months before paying them is abominable. Abide by the rules of business.

BUSINESS WORK DELEGATION

Exodus 18:18

Delegation is all about people and is focused on results rather than the methodology and approach. It validates individual's responsibility and ownership of result/s. This is a working tool of an entrepreneur.

NEED FOR WORK DELEGATION

"You will surely wear out both yourself and this people with you, for the thing is too heavy for you; you are not able to perform it all by yourself."
Exodus 18:18

Work delegation is very important in everything that pertains to business and management. The scripture above acknowledged that one may wear out if he runs the business all alone. The principle of work delegation is not a new management jargon as you may think; rather it is one of the divine management principles in God's word. If you study the entire account of Exodus chapter 18 you will discover that Jethro, Moses father-in-law is an astute management guru to have put forward the theory of delegation of work as at the time in question. To manage your business effectively, it is very important you borrow a leaf from the above management advice.

Delegation is simply getting the right help required, when you need it most for effective result.

Obviously, there is a limit to what one can do or accomplish on personal effort. Delegation is the skill that you have to acquire to achieve business success. Work delegation assists to bring other people on board to share in business burden particularly in areas where one is lacking in skills and knowledge. Effective delegation of duty entails giving clear, succinct lessons of how, when, where and what to be done to someone in order to achieve a desired result. It also involves providing maximum support to the individual concerned based on needs. It is all about people and is focused on results rather than the methodology and approach. It validates individual's responsibility and ownership of result/s.

Irrespective of the good reasons to delegation of work in business; many people even you and I had chosen not to do so for reasons best known to us. Many if not all feel it takes too much time, effort and other visible/invisible resources and they could do it better by themselves. The Bible says; 'You will surely wear out.' When you become master/madam do all in your office and business you are storing and sitting on explosives that will destroy your achievements. Many business owners have collapsed their business because of insecurity and failure to implement duty/work delegation. In your office and personal life let go, delegate or out-source.

Delegation is an important management skill that will help sustain business efforts. But if you don't delegate, you will get to the point where you will destroy what you have worked hard for. For effectiveness and efficiency in work delegation, you have to decide on what to delegate and what not to; find the right person to delegate to and provide detailed explanation of the purpose of the task and your expectation to the person; provide adequate resources both in human, financial and technical required for the task; and finally, reward the effort so that you can continue to enjoy the patronage of your subordinates or network group. Do you practice work delegation?

I'M NOT RESPONSIBLE

Ezra 10:4

Accepting responsibility, correction and being accountable make one a wise, trustworthy, valuable and vital asset to the company.

DENYING RESPONSIBILITY

"Arise, for it is your duty, and we are with you. Be strong {and} brave and do it." Ezra 10:4

This matter or work is your duty, yes! It's mine. This is a sign of boldness and a courageous mind. Too many of us often deny taking charge or accepting responsibility of our action/s in the workplace.

As a business owner/manager or staff you have to accept your mistakes and inappropriate action in the office when called upon. It is of no benefit to give long explanations of what happened just to be exonerated. There is no justification for any mistake committed in the line of duty; rather accept it is your responsibility.

The most valuable thing to do is to admit fault and find appropriate corrective measures to it. In any business environment the moment you learn to admit your responsibility your supervisor or boss will build confidence in you. The bible says, "A wise son heeds [and is the fruit of] his father's instruction {and} correction, but a scoffer listens not to rebuke" Proverbs 13:1. In other words, accepting responsibility, correction and being accountable makes one a wise, trustworthy, valuable and vital asset to the company.

Therefore, when a staff or worker admits mistakes the Scripture says, "We are with you. Be strong {and} brave and do it." Undoubtedly, the management is with you to rectify the outstanding issues. Henceforth, be courageous, strong and act with boldness because you are not alone. Never deny your duty and find reasons to put blames on someone. Standup in your office and say yes, it's my fault and I am working around it to solve the problem. Have you ever denied being responsible?

LACK OF BUSINESS UNDERSTANDING

Proverbs 4:7

Business negotiations require wisdom, knowledge and understanding to manoeuvre. Understanding is shared intellectual alignment for efficient business decision.

THE ESSENCE OF GOOD JUDGEMENT

"The beginning of Wisdom is: get Wisdom (skillful and godly Wisdom)! [For skillful {and} godly Wisdom is the principal thing.] And with all you have gotten, get understanding (discernment, comprehension, and interpretation)" Proverbs 4:7

Businesses are not driven by the quantum of cash one has at his disposal. There are intricacies surrounding small and medium scale business at the local and international level. Business owners/managers should continually educate themselves. They should attend seminars, workshops and presentations. Also conduct a lot of research about the business segment they find themselves into. Importantly, understanding is an indispensible value in today's business.

The Scripture posits that wisdom is the principal thing in business and not only having the relevant knowledge and experience, but the right application of that knowledge and experience for better outcome. It involves proper business judgment.

Today's business places more emphases on the value of understanding of business philosophy, market trend and segmentation and customers' behaviour. This may cost enormous resources to accomplish but it is worth the cost for your business to be competitive.

Education is very vital and valuable in this regard. "In whatever you are getting, get understanding." Business negotiations require wisdom, knowledge and understanding to manoeuvre. Understanding of competitors' business positions and strategies support sound business decision and judgment. The above verse amplified the value of understanding which is- shared intellectual alignment for efficient business decision or otherwise.

Therefore, make an honest effort to be a learner in order to create business value to employees, customers and other stakeholders. Always learn how to apply the right knowledge in business and life. Do you lack understanding of your business?

BUSINESS ETHICS

Matthew 7:12

Ethics underscores intellectual and emotional values unconsciously implemented in our daily activities. Business ethics circles around the moral judgments about what is right and what is wrong.

THE GOLDEN RULE--BUSINESS ETHICS

"So then, whatever you desire that others would do to {and} for you, even so do also to {and} for them, for this is (sums up) the Law and the Prophets."
Matthew 7:12

In the contemporary business world, the success of any business notwithstanding the size goes beyond its profitability and financial statements. However, organizational architecture, business management philosophy and ethics play vital roles in its long-term success. Above all, business ethics stands out as the prime factor of business sustainability.

The golden rule is laid out as the above verse suggests 'do to others whatever you wish them to do to you.' Therefore, business ethics circles around the moral judgments about what is right and what is wrong. In the business context, they are decided and established by each company or organization which anchors the decisions that anyone in the business makes.

Business owners and managers should have clear understanding that God's approved business must be strictly founded on firm ethics and social responsibility. As business owners/managers when we put ourselves into the position of our customers and vendors; we'll understand why they need to be treated better than we do. For instance, if you are to be a customer to your business outfit would you like the manner and way you return phone calls, reply emails; attend to customer's problems, and your frontline manager's attitude and response to people?

In business operation let 'yes be yes and no be no.' Customers should know you for something reputable. Think of a unique way of solving different customer's problem/s. Today, have a holistic view of your business. How can you tailor your products and services to a unique need of your customer? Secondly, how can you make 20% of your customers feel valued? Pareto principle 80-20 rule says, 80% of business revenue comes from 20% of the customers. This could only be achieved when you do to your customers, what you wish another business at the other side of the road will do to you as their customer.

Therefore, consistent business ethics and social responsibility brings positive public image, short and long term profit, customer loyalty and increased employee morale. Does your business lacks ethics?

BRAINPOWER A BUSINESS TOOL

Isaiah 1: 18 NET

Brainstorming is a procedure that uses team collaboration to generate ideas and systematically apply them to the advantage of the business to remain competitive. Lester Thurow asserts the view that the industries we are competing for - the industries of the future - are all based on brainpower.

TEAM BRAINSTORMING

"Come; let's consider your options;" Isaiah 1: 18 NET

Business growth is a product of brainstorming, research and development, meticulous interpretation and applications of findings. Therefore, in every structured business, organization or institution the use of brainstorming is indispensible. The business team cannot produce effective result if they throw aside the concept of brainstorming in their effort to strategize for product innovation. Brainstorming is a procedure that uses team collaboration to generate ideas and systematically apply them to the advantage of the business. The team in collaboration with the management should brainstorm from time to time on various ways of attracting customers and the possible ways of retaining them. Remember that there is no one size fits all in this, your environment and nature of business determine what you have to do.

Brainstorming works only:

- When there is a cross-functional business team

- When each team member is genuinely encouraged to say his idea without an attack.

- When purpose and goal are clearly defined by the parties.

- When team members unanimously discuss and agree on one idea irrespective of who proposed it.

In view of this, the team should produce in no time diverse ideas and solutions to improve customers' relation and retention rate. "Come, let's consider your options;" says the Lord..... Isaiah 1:18, (New English Translation). In other words, we are asked to come together and brainstorm for a way forward in serving customers better than before. How often does your business team brainstorm?

ROOT CAUSE OF BUSINESS SUCCESS

1 Corinthians 15:58

What keeps a business owner pursuing the business vision despite failures or challenges is perseverance. The ability to adapt to business changes with perseverance underscores success in business.

DON'T QUIT YOUR BUSINESS

"Therefore, my beloved brethren, be firm (steadfast), immovable, always abounding in the work of the Lord [always being superior, excelling, doing more than enough in the service of the Lord], knowing {and} being continually aware that your labor in the Lord is not futile [it is never wasted or to no purpose]." 1 Corinthians 15:58

The opening chapter of this book started with "Deliberating over Past Business Failures and Never Submit to Past Failures." Business is a function of risk. Therefore, the root cause of business success is equally a function of persistence, commitment, determination, and positive self-worth channeled toward a predetermined course. What keeps a business owner pursuing the business vision despite failures or challenges is perseverance.

Persistence is defined as absolute refusal to submit to failures and discouragement in business and life in general. It is the quality that allows an entrepreneur to continue on his business goals and objectives even though it is difficult or opposed by other business associates. The Scripture above says, "My beloved brethren, be firm (steadfast), immovable, always abounding in the work- knowing (and) being continually aware that your labor in the Lord is not futile (it is never wasted or to no purpose)." Never quit as long as you are on the right course. "Energy and persistence conquer all things" says Benjamin Franklin.

Business is not for the chicken-hearted minds but is for the strong. Therefore, the application of persistence in business is what distinguishes between those who are successful and those who fail. According to Thomas A. Edison "Our greatest weakness lies in giving up. The most certain way to succeed is always to try just one more time." The patience and tenacity to stretch one more time is the hard nut to crack. Are you persistent with the task and project before you? What about your business goals and vision? The Bible asserts "And let us not lose heart {and} grow weary {and} faint in acting nobly {and} doing right, for in due time {and} at the appointed season we shall reap, if we do not loosen {and} relax our courage {and} faint" Galatians 6:9. When the going gets tough just remember at the appointed season/time in business, we shall reap, if we do not loosen and relax our courage and commitment to the corporate vision.

To win the business race, there is need for a defined business goal and vision. The business actor has to remain focused and motivated knowing that there are inevitable obstacles and setbacks on the way. The ability to adapt to business changes with perseverance underscores success in business. Napoleon Hill asserts that "The most interesting thing about a postage stamp is the persistence with which it sticks to its job." Always be persistent to your business vision, is closer than imagined.

SCRIPTURES FOR BUSINESS SUCCESS

Below are infallible biblical references that guarantee business success if properly applied. There is nothing one can do without the word of God. Always, study and meditate these and make them your daily business bread; it shall prosper you in whatever and wherever you go. "I know that whatever God does it shall be forever..." (Ecclesiastes 3: 14). That is to say, business success comes from God and is forever and impregnable.

Also, business accountability, leadership, communication, ethics and competition have great root of success embedded in the word of God.

Accountability in Business

1 You shall not defraud {or} oppress your neighbor or rob him; the wages of a hired servant shall not remain with you all night until morning. **Leviticus 19:13**

2 And be like men who are waiting for their master to return home from the marriage feast, so that when he returns from the wedding and comes and knocks, they may open to him immediately. **Luke 12:36**

3 If the clouds are full of rain, they empty themselves upon the earth; and if a tree falls toward the south or toward the north, in the place where the tree falls, there it will lie. **Ecclesiastes 11:3**

4 So teach us to number our days, that we may get us a heart of wisdom. **Psalm 90:12**

5 You hypocrite, first get the beam of timber out of your own eye, and then you will see clearly to take the tiny particle out of your brother's eye. **Matthew 7:5**

6 He who is loose {and} slack in his work is brother to him who is a destroyer {and} {he who does not use his endeavors to heal himself is brother to him who commits suicide}. **Proverbs 18:9**

7 Arise, for it is your duty, and we are with you. Be

strong {and} brave and do it. **Ezra 10:4**

8 There are those who [generously] scatter abroad, and yet increase more; there are those who withhold more than is fitting {or} what is justly due, but it results only in want. **Proverbs 11:24**

9 [Wisdom] walk in the way of righteousness (moral and spiritual rectitude in every area and relation), in the midst of the paths of justice, That I may cause those who love me to inherit [true] riches and that I may fill their treasuries **Proverbs 8:20-21**

10 From the fruit of his words a man shall be satisfied with good, and the work of a man's hands shall come back to him [as a harvest]. **Proverbs 12:14**

11 A WISE son heeds [and is the fruit of] his father's instruction {and} correction, but a scoffer listens not to rebuke. **Proverbs 13:1**

12 Withhold not good from those to whom it is due [its rightful owners], when it is in the power of your

hand to do it. Do not say to your neighbor, Go, and come again; and tomorrow I will give it--when you have it with you. **Proverbs 3:27-28**

Leadership in Business

1 I also held fast to the work on this wall; and we bought no land. And all my servants were gathered there for the work. **Nehemiah 5:16**

2 Even a child is known by his acts, whether [or not] what he does is pure and right. **Proverbs 20:11**

3 Loving-kindness {and} mercy, truth {and} faithfulness, preserve the king, and his throne is upheld by [the people's] loyalty. **Proverbs 20:28**

4 But Moses' hands were heavy {and} grew weary. So [the other men] took a stone and put it under him and he sat on it. Then Aaron and Hur held up his hands, one on one side and one on the other side; so his hands were steady until the going down of the sun. **Exodus 17:12**

5 Reuben, you are my firstborn, my might, the

beginning (the firstfruits) of my manly strength {and} vigor; [your birthright gave you] the preeminence in dignity and the preeminence in power. But unstable {and} boiling over like water, you shall not excel {and} have the preeminence [of the firstborn], because you went to your father's bed; you defiled it--he went to my couch! **Gen 49:3-4**

Ethics in Business

1 You shall do no unrighteousness in judgment, in measures of length or weight or quantity. You shall have accurate {and} just balances, just weights, just ephah and hin measures. I am the Lord your God, Who brought you out of the land of Egypt. **Leviticus 19:35-36**

2 IF ANYONE sins in that he is sworn to testify and has knowledge of the matter, either by seeing or hearing of it, but fails to report it, then he shall bear his iniquity {and} willfulness. **Leviticus 5:1**

3 Good understanding wins favor, but the way of the transgressor is hard [like the barren, dry soil or the

impassable swamp] **Proverbs 13:15**

4 Let your Yes be simply Yes, and your No be simply No; anything more than that comes from the evil one. **Matthew 5:37**

5 Let each of you esteem {and} look upon {and} be concerned for not [merely] his own interests, but also each for the interests of others. **Philippians 2:4**

6 If a man vows a vow to the Lord or swears an oath to bind himself by a pledge, he shall not break {and} profane his word; he shall do according to all that proceeds out of his mouth. **Numbers 30:2**

7 So then, whatever you desire that others would do to {and} for you, even so do also to {and} for them, for this is (sums up) the Law and the Prophets. **Matthew 7:12**

Competition in Business

1 David said to Saul, Let no man's heart fail because of this Philistine; your servant will go out and fight with him. **1 Samuel 17:32**

2 Draw for yourself the water [necessary] for a [long continued] siege, make strong your fortresses! Go down into the clay pits and trample the mortar; make ready the brickkiln [to burn bricks for the bulwarks]! **Nahum 3:14**

3 For by wise counsel you can wage your war, and in an abundance of counselors there is victory {and} safety, **Proverb 24:6**

4 For which of you, wishing to build a farm building, does not first sit down and calculate the cost [to see] whether he has sufficient means to finish it? Or what king, going out to engage in conflict with another king, will not first sit down and consider {and} take counsel whether he is able with ten thousand [men] to meet him who comes against him with twenty thousand? **Luke 14:28, 31**

5 Send men to explore {and} scout out [for yourselves] the land of Canaan, which I give to the Israelites. From each tribe of their fathers you shall send a man, everyone a leader {or} head among

them. **Numbers 13:2**

6 [Put first things first.] Prepare your work outside
and get it ready for yourself in the field; and
afterward build your house {and} establish a home.
Proverbs 24:27

Communication in Business

1 Then I said to them, You see the bad situation we
are in--how Jerusalem lies in ruins, and its gates are
burned with fire. Come, let us build up the wall of
Jerusalem, that we may no longer be a disgrace.
Nehemiah 2:17

2 All this the Lord made me understand by the
writing by His hand upon me, all the work to be
done according to the plan. **1 Chronicles 28:19**

3 Let no foul {or} polluting language, {nor} evil
word {nor} unwholesome {or} worthless talk [ever]
come out of your mouth, but only such [speech] as is
good {and} beneficial to the spiritual progress of
others, as is fitting to the need {and} the occasion,

that it may be a blessing {and} give grace (God's favor) to those who hear it. **Ephesians 4:29**

4 But if the watchman sees the sword coming and does not blow the trumpet and the people are not warned, and the sword comes and takes any one of them, he is taken away in {and} for his perversity {and} iniquity, but his blood will I require at the watchman's hand. **Ezek1el 33:6**

5 Understand [this], my beloved brethren. Let every man be quick to hear [a ready listener], slow to speak, slow to take offense {and} to get angry. **James 1:19**

6 Concerning this we have much to say which is hard to explain, since you have become dull in your [spiritual] hearing {and} sluggish [even slothful in achieving spiritual insight]. **Hebrews 5:11**

OTHER BIBLE VERSES ABOUT BUSINESS

1 And the Lord God took the man and put him in the Garden of Eden to tend and guard {and} keep it. **Genesis 2:15**

2 Six days you shall do your work, but the seventh day you shall rest and keep Sabbath, that your ox and your donkey may rest, and the son of your bondwoman, and the alien, may be refreshed. **Exodus 23:12**

3 He has filled them with wisdom of heart {and} ability to do all manner of craftsmanship, of the engraver, of the skillful workman, of the embroiderer in blue, purple, and scarlet [stuff] and in fine linen, and of the weaver, even of those who do or design any skilled work. **Exodus 35:35**

4 You shall not defraud {or} oppress your neighbor or rob him; the wages of a hired servant shall not remain with you all night until morning. **Leviticus 19:13**

5 You shall not have in your bag true and false weights, a large and a small. You shall not have in your house true and false measures, a large and a small. But you shall have a perfect and just weight and a perfect and just measure, that your days may be prolonged in the land which the Lord your God gives you. **Deuteronomy 25:13-15**

6 My servants, both men and women, sometimes had problems. But if they spoke to me about their problems, I always answered them fairly. God might ask me questions about that. But if I had not listened to them, I could not have answered honestly. **Job 31: 13-14 EasyEnglish**

7 For they all wanted to frighten us, thinking, their hands will be so weak that the work will not be done. But now strengthen my hands! **Nehemiah 6:9**

8 It is well with the man who deals generously and lends, who conducts his affairs with justice. **Psalm 112:5**

9 He becomes poor who works with a slack {and} idle hand, but the hand of the diligent makes rich. **Proverbs 10:4**

10 The Lord detests dishonest scales, but accurate weights find favor with him. **Proverbs 11:1 NIV**

11 The appetite of the sluggard craves and gets nothing, but the appetite of the diligent is abundantly supplied. **Proverbs 13:4**

12 Wealth [not earned but] won in haste {or} unjustly {or} from the production of things for vain {or} detrimental use [such riches] will dwindle away, but he who gathers little by little will increase [his riches]. **Proverbs 13:11**

13 Better is a little with righteousness (uprightness in every area and relation and right standing with God) than great revenues with injustice. **Proverbs 16:8**

14 Plan of the persistent surely lead to productivity, but all who are hasty will surely become poor. **Proverbs 21:5 ISV**

15 Whoever oppresses the poor to enrich himself and whoever gives gifts to the wealthy will yield only loss. **Proverbs 22:16 ISV**

16 What the lazy person craves will kill him, because his hands refuse to work. **Proverbs 21:25 ISV**

17 Woe to him who builds his house by unrighteousness and his [upper] chambers by injustice, who uses his neighbor's service without wages and does not give him his pay [for his work], **17 Jeremiah 22:13**

18 You shall not muzzle an ox when it is treading out the grain, and again, The laborer is worthy of his hire. **1Timothy 5:18**

19 He who is faithful in a very little [thing] is faithful also in much, and he who is dishonest {and} unjust in a very little [thing] is dishonest {and} unjust also in much. **Luke 16:10**

20 You masters, act on the same [principle] toward them and give up threatening {and} using violent {and} abusive words, knowing that He Who is both their Master and yours is in heaven, and that there is no respect of persons (no partiality) with Him. **Ephesians 6:9**

21 MASTERS, [on your part] deal with your slaves justly and fairly, knowing that also you have a Master in heaven. **Colossians 4:1**

22 Whatever may be your task, work at it heartily (from the soul), as [something done] for the Lord and not for men. **Colossians 3:23**

Notes

Amplified Bible, 1987 edition. The Lockman Foundation La Habra CA 90631. www.lockman.org

David Lewis. "10-Minute Time and Stress Management" Judy Piatkus (Publishers) Ltd. London. 1995.

John C. Maxwell. "The 21 Irrefutable Laws of Leadership, Follow Them and People Will Follow You" Revised and Updated 10th Anniversary Edition. Thomas Nelson, Inc. 1998 and 2007.

Nguzo C. Uche. "The Roaring Success" Createspace, USA. 2015.

Steve Marr. "Proverbs for Business" Revell, division of Baker Publishing Group. 2001.

AUTHOR'S RECOMMENDATION

Every question/s in each page, and chapter is meant for you to honestly provide an answer. Please don't move to the next page or chapter without an in-depth answers to guide your business in the right direction.

Any answer provided should not end on paper or in the drawer rather it should be translated and implemented in the business with total commitment. Despite the position you occupy whether an employer or employee be diligent and truthful as integrity pays.

God's Legal Tender

Dr. Nguzo C. Uche

God's Legal Tender is a book designed for all Christians and those who teach faith concepts and principles either at churches, schools, and homes. The concept of faith has been conceived and misinterpreted by many in our generation. The book differentiates between believe and faith through faith equation, faith lever and faith process. It explains how faith transformation vectors will activate your faith in God and its application. Also, it highlights in details what faith viruses are, how to identify and cure them.

ISBN-13: 978-1503141513.

Paperback. 90 pages.

Published by CreateSpace, USA

Dynamic Church Visitors Follow-up Strategy

Dr. Nguzo C. Uche

All functional organizations like the church need a structured and effective visitors' follow-up strategy. This book presents a model for church leaders and administrators to use in winning and retaining first time visitors. It has a practical approach to church visitors' team formation, follow-up methods, monitoring and evaluation plan; visitors' integration, retention and continuous process improvement strategies, designed to work for all churches irrespective of size.

ISBN-13: 978-1511593946
Paperback. 66 pages
Published by CreateSpace, USA

ISBN-13: 978-1512329193
Paperback: 132 pages
Published by CreateSpace, USA

The Roaring Success reveals the Divine purpose of God concerning your good success He promised. Success is a product of obedience to the laws and principles of God and that of life. It is the ultimate will of God to see that you succeed for His reputation and for your life to shine as a light to others. This book is a guide that teaches you not just how to be successful through God's word, but how to manage your success beyond the present. It is entirely based on God's profound law of success enshrined in the Bible. The Roaring Success is a material for self-empowerment and a tool to make yourself prosperous not depending on anyone if you abide by His word. Success is Bible based.

Nguzo C. Uche

www.ingramcontent.com/pod-product-compliance
Lightning Source LLC
Chambersburg PA
CBHW070028210526
45170CB00012B/466